INSPIRATIONS THAT COME FROM THE MORNING VIEW

Inspirations that Come from the Morning View

BRENDA G. WILSON BILLINGS

LOWBAR
PUBLISHING COMPANY

905 South Douglas Avenue • Nashville, Tennessee 37204
Phone: 615-972-2842
E-mail: Lowbarpublishingcompany@gmail.com
Web site: www.Lowbarbookstore.com

Copyright © 2017 Brenda G. Wilson Billings

No part of this book may be reproduced or transmitted in any form or by any means—graphic, electronic, or mechanical, including photocopying, recording, taping, or by any information storage retrieval system—without the permission, in writing, of the publisher or author.

Lowbar Publishing Company
905 S. Douglas Ave.
Nashville, Tennessee 37204
615-972-2842
Lowbarpublishingcompany@gmail.com
www.Lowbarbookstore.com

Content Editor: Calvin C. Barlow Jr.
Photos by Calvin C. Barlow Jr.
Editor: Honey B. Higgins
Graphic and Cover Design Artist: Norah S. Branch

Unless otherwise noted, Scripture references in this book are taken from the King James Version of the Holy Bible.

Printed in the United States of America.
ISBN: 978-0-9969432-3-9

For additional information or to contact the author for workshops or seminars, please call 313-910-7677, or e-mail us: Lowbarpublishingcompany@gmail.com

Dickie Wilson Jr.

To my parents, Reverend and Mrs. J. C. Barnes; brothers—Michael Barnes, Reverend Dr. Myron D. Barnes; son, James Barnes; granddaughter, Jasha Barnes; sisters-in-law—Ollie and Sharon Halls; and other beloved family members. Special recognition goes to my deceased husband, Dickie Wilson Jr., and my current husband, Kevin Billings.

Kevin Billings

Table of Contents

Foreword 9
Inspired Words 10
    Pastor Carr 10
    The Good Days 12
    God 14
    The Lord Is So Good 16
    Happy Mother's Day 18
    Daniel in the Lions' Den 20
    Every Little Blessing 22
    Thank You, Lord 24
    What a Wonderful God 26
    There Is Something about Prayer 28
    You Are My Child 30
    Daily Walking with Jesus 32
    Thank You, Lord (A Sonnet) 34
    Christ, He Died 36
    Jesus 38
    Watching over Us 40
    Daily Talking to Jesus 42
    Lord, I Put My Trust in You 44
    God Is a Deliverer 46

In This Day and Age 48
So Many Things 50
Jesus Is a Wonderful Friend 52
Life 54
Let's Give God the Glory 56
To My Brother on Father's Day 58
Cherish Spring 60
A Mother 62
There May Be Tears 64

SOMETIMES 66

Sonnet A 68
Sonnet B 68
Sonnet C 69
Sonnet D 70
Sonnet E 71
Sonnet F 72
Sonnet G 73
Sonnet H 74
Sonnet I 75
Sonnet J 76
Sonnet K 77
Sonnet L 78
Sonnet M 79

Foreword

A dawning of a new day, a new season, and a new way of seeing yourself is finally here in this awesome and incredible, inspirational color masterpiece. This wonderful book has been more than an enjoyed reading—it has been refreshing and reviving, and it has certainly refueled my soul. *Inspirations that Come from the Morning View* has encouraged my beating heart and has helped me get through some tough times; it has also helped me to heal old wounds that had me bound. Having read this book, I gained a sense of renewal that my day starts the way "I say" and "see" it.

Scripture tells us that "his anger endureth but a moment; in his favour is life: weeping may endure for a night, but joy cometh in the morning" (Psalm 30:5).

Brenda Billings, who has gone through so many ups and downs of life, reminds us that joy is on schedule if we just continue to remain focused and look for all the great and good things that come out of and from the *Morning View*.

Dr. A. Arbutus Carr Jr., D.D.
Morning View Missionary Baptist Church
5646 Lawton St.
Detroit, MI 48208

Pastor Carr

*Let the elders that rule well
be counted worthy of double honour,
especially they who labour in the word and doctrine.*

(1 Timothy 5:17)

Pastor Carr

When God sent us Reverend Carr,

He sent us more than a gem;

He sent us someone special—to represent Him.

He could have sent us diamonds, or the highest of anything;

But, He chose a wonderful preacher to lift His holy name.

As Christmastime approaches

we celebrate our Savior's birth;

And Reverend Carr will be preaching,

On how Christ came here to earth.

Dr. Carr listens to all of our ailments,

Yet, he is not an M.D.;

And, as we share him,

Jesus leads us to our victory.

So, may you be blessed, Reverend Carr,

Because we know you have a hard task;

And we thank God for you:

May the love for you, from Morning View,

Always, always last.

The Good Days

*So teach us to number our days,
that we may apply our hearts unto wisdom.*

(Psalm 90:12)

The Good Days

I remember those days:

When the grass was green,

The sky was blue,

The sun was shining—

And today is like that.

Where God reigns over the whole universe,

And I'm still here;

Still—in the land of the living.

What a great feeling:

To see, to feel, and to know that those days are still here.

God

The earth is the Lord's, and the fulness thereof; the world, and they that dwell therein.

(Psalm 24:1)

God

How can I explain all the beautiful things

that God has done for me?

He gave me breath,

He gave me life,

He gave me the victory.

In times of trouble, He has been with me:

Through the storms,

Through hell and rain,

He has been my Father, Mother, Sister, and Brother.

His love is Eternal.

The Lord Is So Good

*My help cometh from the L*ORD*,
which made heaven and earth.*

(Psalm 121:2)

The Lord Is So Good

The Lord is so good,

He shows me the way—

To live in a world of stress each day.

And every problem I own,

He solves them all until stress is gone.

His Word is embedded deep down within,

And sorrows of this old world will end.

I can't help but to praise Him in my own way,

For He blesses me and keeps me from day to day.

Happy Mother's Day

*She openeth her mouth with wisdom;
and in her tongue is the law of kindness.
She looketh well to the ways of her household,
and eateth not the bread of idleness.*

(Proverbs 31:26-27)

Happy Mother's Day

May your Mother's Day be filled with lots of happiness,

And may all your children know that

It's because of you they are blessed.

May your day be joyous,

From beginning to end.

And may knowing that you are loved

Rejuvenate you once again.

Daniel in the Lions' Den

*Then the king commanded, and they brought Daniel,
and cast him into the den of lions.
Now the king spake and said unto Daniel,
Thy God whom thou servest continually,
he will deliver thee.*

(Daniel 6:16)

Daniel in the Lions' Den

Sometimes I wonder how fearful it would have been,
For Daniel in the lions' den.
Then I look back at how He spared my life—
Through it all,
And with all of the trouble that I've been in,
He watched over me just like Daniel in the lions' den.
Then, He set me free from the lion's mouth.
He gave me joy—joy divine,
Let me put my past behind:
It was to me like Daniel in the lions' den.

Every Little Blessing

Blessed be the God and Father of our Lord Jesus Christ, who hath blessed us with all spiritual blessings in heavenly places in Christ.

(Ephesians 1:3)

Every Little Blessing

Every little blessing is a big blessing, too,
Living and breathing your whole life through;
So many things for granted we take,
This is the biggest mistake we can make.
Having seeing eyes or being able to talk,
Being able to move around and walk.
All of God's blessings are precious, you see,
A big little blessing from God to me.

Thank You, Lord

*Sing unto the LORD, O ye saints of his,
and give thanks at the remembrance of his holiness.*

(Psalm 30:4)

Thank You, Lord

Thank You, Lord, for dying for me,
For loving me enough that I might believe.
Thank You, Lord, for answering each prayer,
For showing me love and showing You care.
I can't praise You enough for the things You have done,
But my heart appreciates all the victories we have won.
Thank You, Lord, for strength and health,
For everything You've given to me;
Each blessing is wealth,
Thank You—One in Three.

What a Wonderful God

*I will praise thee; for I am fearfully and wonderfully made:
marvellous are thy works;
and that my soul knoweth right well.*

(Psalm 139:14)

What a Wonderful God

What a wonderful God we serve,

He's patient as can be;

He's kind, sweet, and loving,

And He's always there for me.

A father or a mother,

He can be both, you see!

A doctor or a lawyer,

He's almighty, yes, indeed.

Jesus died upon the Cross,

To save us from our sins.

He came between God and us

To help us make amends.

So, having a wonderful God is precious and worthwhile;

His grace saved us and gave us worth,

And lets each of us be His child.

There Is Something about Prayer

Give ear to my prayer, O God;
and hide not thyself from my supplication.

(Psalm 55:1)

There Is Something about Prayer

There is something about prayer,

And the power of prayer;

And when you least expect it,

My Master will be there—

Kneeling at His throne.

And having God,

To answer each problem,

That you own:

Jesus!

He will answer,

And supply your every need,

There is something about God

That will help you to succeed.

You Are My Child

What is man, that thou art mindful of him? and the son of man, that thou visitest him?

(Psalm 8:4)

You Are My Child

You are my child that I have not seen;

Yet, I know that you are beautiful,

Because you're a part of me.

As none have seen God before,

We love Him and trust Him just the same.

In His image,

I am beautiful—

And so is He.

Daily Walking with Jesus

And I will walk among you, and will be your God, and ye shall be my people.

(Leviticus 26:12)

Daily Walking with Jesus

Daily walking with Jesus

Means so much to me;

Having Him there to guide me,

Means I can be free.

Wrapped up, with His arms around me,

We are quite a team;

Daily walking with Jesus

Means so much to me.

Thank You, Lord (A Sonnet)

*Enter into his gates with thanksgiving,
and into his courts with praise: be thankful unto him,
and bless his name.*

(Psalm 100:4)

Thank You, Lord (A Sonnet)

Thank You, Lord, for everything,

Every day,

Each blessing,

You bring with hope and joy:

For the love You give,

And sparing everyone to live;

For forgiving us of sin and shame,

For sending the sunshine and the rain.

To You we owe our every praise—

Thank You, Lord, for blessing all of our days.

Christ, He Died

*But God commendeth his love toward us,
in that, while we were yet sinners,
Christ died for us.*

(Romans 5:8)

Christ, He Died

Christ, He died for you and me,

He gave His life on Calvary's tree:

That young and old,

Rich and poor,

Could have sweet life in eternity;

With Him as our Master,

He said that He would receive us

In a place He is preparing to be with us . . .

My Jesus!

Jesus

For the wages of sin is death; but the gift of God is eternal life through Jesus Christ our Lord.

(Romans 6:23)

Jesus

Jesus,

He came to the world just to save a wretch like me.

He lived,

Then He gave His life out on Calvary.

Calvary's tree!

Where they pierced Him in His precious side,

And the blood came streaming down.

He died,

In your place and mine,

That we wouldn't be hell-bound.

Jesus!

There is so much power in His name;

How precious He is to me!

His love goes beyond anyone else—

He made it where salvation would be free.

Watching over Us

*I will lift up mine eyes unto the hills,
from whence cometh my help.
My help cometh from the L<small>ORD</small>,
which made heaven and earth.
He will not suffer thy foot to be moved:
he that keepeth thee will not slumber.*

(Psalm 121:1-3)

Watching over Us

For watching over us
During the nights and days,
And keeping us in Your care;
For blessing our lives every day,
For always being there.
For loving us despite our sin,
And helping us to succeed;
I thank You, God, for all You've done,
For each and every deed.

Daily Talking to Jesus

*Thy word is a lamp unto my feet,
and a light unto my path.*

(Psalm 119:105)

Daily Talking to Jesus

Daily talking to Jesus
Leads me along my way;
Having Him for a teacher
Helps me not to stray.
Lovingly, He gently guides me,
No matter come what may;
He is my provider and shelter—
Each and every day.

Lord, I Put My Trust in You

Trust in the L<small>ORD</small> with all thine heart; and lean not unto thine own understanding. In all thy ways acknowledge him, and he shall direct thy paths.

(Proverbs 3:5-6)

Lord, I Put My Trust in You

Lord, I put my trust in You,

Praying that You will see me through.

When all else around me is in distress,

I thank You, Lord, for joy and happiness.

When fear sometimes wants to control,

My faith is all I know.

And, somehow that mustard seed I own,

Will grow until it's fully grown.

My love for You is strong, I know,

But weak sometimes, it takes a toll.

Please bless me and my loved ones, too,

And daily I'll learn to trust in You.

God Is a Deliverer

Thou art my hiding place; thou shalt preserve me from trouble; thou shalt compass me about with songs of deliverance.

(Psalm 32:7)

God Is a Deliverer

God is a deliverer at best;

If you just reach out to Him,

He will do the rest.

He is a doctor and a friend;

He will heal you again and again.

Sickness comes in all different forms;

You just need to ask Him—

And miracles He will perform.

We all need Him for each breath we breathe;

He will deliver us from our sickness and grief.

Just call on Jesus when you need a friend,

For He promised to be with us—even to the end.

In This Day and Age

Hear me when I call, O God of my righteousness: thou hast enlarged me when I was in distress; have mercy upon me, and hear my prayer.

(Psalm 4:1)

In This Day and Age

In this day and age,

When nobody answers their phone,

You can call on the name of Jesus,

He will show you that you are not alone.

When you call a so-called friend,

And they won't pick up—because of "caller I.D.":

You don't have to worry Jesus,

All you have to do is believe.

As you open your Bible,

And turn off the TV,

You can hear what the Master says,

And let your mind be free.

So Many Things

And call upon me in the day of trouble: I will deliver thee, and thou shalt glorify me.

(Psalm 50:15)

So Many Things

So many things may happen—
Sickness, death, and trouble are three;
But you will learn to accept them all,
For you will never be free from them at all.
Once you accept what happens,
You're on the road to recovery;
But if you can't accept it,
You can't reach your victory.
Jesus can carry our burdens,
But some things we have to do;
Learn to accept whatever comes,
And God will see you through.

Jesus Is a Wonderful Friend

A man that hath friends must shew himself friendly: and there is a friend that sticketh closer than a brother.

(Proverbs 18:24)

Jesus Is a Wonderful Friend

Jesus is a wonderful friend,

And never too busy;

And as He holds the whole world in His hands,

He always has time for me.

So, as you get on your knees,

And have a fervent prayer;

You'll soon realize,

It's most important when Jesus is there.

He will give you insight,

Into how to treat your fellow man;

And any kind of miracle

Is in His hand.

So, let everybody be busy,

And that's okay, too;

But never forget that

It was God who brought you through.

Life

*For God so loved the world,
that he gave his only begotten Son,
that whosoever believeth in him should not perish,
but have everlasting life.*

(John 3:16)

Life

Life is a flower in full bloom,

Spreading its fragrance in the midst of June.

Born as a bud in the warm spring shower,

Dried in the fall in the autumn hour.

Then comes snow,

To take away its peaceful resting—

And eternal way,

We cannot see or understand death stings.

But by and by,

It will soon be spring.

Let's Give God the Glory

*Praise ye the LORD. Praise the LORD, O my soul.
While I live will I praise the LORD:
I will sing praises unto my God while I have any being.
Put not your trust in princes, nor in the son of man,
in whom there is no help.*

(Psalm 146:1-3)

Let's Give God the Glory

Let's give God the glory,

For He deserves it all;

Let's sing hallelujah,

For He won't let you fall.

Whether a mother or a father,

Or just a little child;

Jesus is holy,

Lowly, meek, and mild.

Let's praise Him with singing,

And clapping of our hands;

For God is almighty,

And God—He understands.

Jesus, Jesus,

There is power in His name;

And when you find Him for yourself,

You will never be the same.

To My Brother on Father's Day

Let brotherly love continue.

(Hebrews 13:1)

To My Brother on Father's Day

A brother is special,
And not just for a while;
For I love you daily,
Because you always make me smile.
A brother will look out for you,
No matter what comes your way;
So, wishing you on this occasion
A very Happy Father's Day.

Cherish Spring

And God said, Let there be lights in the firmament of the heaven to divide the day from the night; and let them be for signs, and for seasons, and for days, and years.

(Genesis 1:14)

Cherish Spring

Chirping birds, the way they sing,

Letting the world know it's spring.

Trees and flowers are all in bud,

Life is sweet and full of love.

All is in wonder,

Each and every thing,

Praise God above,

And cherish spring.

A Mother

*Honour thy father and mother;
which is the first commandment with promise.*

(Ephesians 6:2)

A Mother

A mother is so precious,

And lovely as a flower;

And each and every day,

She is lovelier by the hour.

A mother is so wondrous,

A kind and gentle soul;

Her virtue and her love

Are felt by young and old.

And not only is she kind,

In word and deed she's love;

A blessing from almighty God,

A blessing from above.

May Mother's Day bring you

Blessings from above;

And may you be content

In the warmth of God's love.

There May Be Tears

*For thou hast delivered my soul from death,
mine eyes from tears, and my feet from falling.*

(Psalm 116:8)

There May Be Tears

There may be tears in our eyes;

But Jesus will be there—

And that is no surprise.

Losing a loved one is so hard;

But He will comfort—

For He is God.

Crossing over is not so bad;

When we know new life will still be had.

God will console each and every one;

On earth and in heaven—

His will be done.

SOMETIMES

Based upon the theme "Sometimes," I present a series of poetic, rhythm-inspired moving thoughts. For identification, they are listed as Sonnet A through Sonnet M.

Sometimes

For his anger endureth but a moment; in his favour is life: weeping may endure for a night, but joy cometh in the morning.

(Psalm 30:5)

SOMETIMES (Sonnet A)

Sometimes,

When I feel all by myself,

I look to the Lord,

To find my way.

Though depressed I may be,

He hears me and comforts me;

I find joy,

Just knowing I'm blessed.

SOMETIMES (Sonnet B)

Sometimes,

When I think about how things are bad,

I just think of how much worse things could be.

Then, I realize how things are good to me.

Sometimes,

When I wonder,

I just put my trust in God;

And, He will make it possible,

To have victories over all of the odds.

SOMETIMES (Sonnet C)

Sometimes,

We feel that because we're sick,

We're being punished;

But, look at the hospitals,

They all are filled:

If we didn't get sick,

Or have any problems,

Then we wouldn't know,

God is real.

He's the healer of all diseases,

He's a comfort to the bereaved;

He's a doctor, lawyer, mother, father, and anything else to us,

If we believe.

God will heal your body,

Just trust in His name;

He loves all of us;

And, what He does for others,

For you, He'll do the same.

SOMETIMES (Sonnet D)

Sometimes,

I'm so amazed by

What God can do for you;

Not only will He make a way,

But He'll see you through.

Sometimes,

My understanding is so irrational;

But God knows our feelings,

And He is in control.

SOMETIMES (Sonnet E)

Sometimes,

Things get so bad,

That you think you want to die;

But that's where Jesus comes in—

To hear your every cry.

Sometimes,

It seems there's no place to turn;

But, Jesus will comfort you,

No matter what concerns you.

Sometimes,

You feel that God is not there;

But, kneel down and ask Him

To answer your prayer.

Don't stop trying,

And don't give up—

Even when life gets rough and tough.

He can heal and He will deliver,

And He will be there just for you;

Just keep praising and praying,

For He will see you through.

SOMETIMES (Sonnet F)

Sometimes,

We have to endure pain;

Sometimes,

We have to live with the sin and shame:

God opens doors for whomever He will;

Sometimes,

We have to swallow a bitter pill.

But, the Lord knows just how much we can bear;

And, His mercy shows that He cares.

And, your midnights will end at dawn;

Sometimes,

We have to remember just where we came from.

The Lord is the light in darkness;

Repent and sin no more,

And you will be blessed.

SOMETIMES (Sonnet G)

Sometimes,

I don't know what to do;

But I believe my Jesus will see me through.

The things I have to bear in life,

I know He'll be there,

And make everything all right.

Sometimes,

Just knowing what He can do,

Is enough to strengthen and comfort me.

So, no matter what the task,

My Jesus' love will forever last.

SOMETIMES (Sonnet H)

Sometimes,

When I think "I can't do,"

Love goes its distance.

When it seems like resistance is at its best,

Love gives you that extra push.

For God loves us,

And He gives us strength to face any incident.

So, if you want to make it through,

Do the things God will have you to do.

SOMETIMES (Sonnet I)

Sometimes,

As I look back over my life,

Memories seem so sad;

But when I think about how God has brought me out,

Then I really don't feel so bad.

It was Him—Jesus—who brought me out;

It was Him—Jesus—without a doubt.

Sometimes,

I look back over my life,

And I can truly say:

God has played an important part in my life,

Each and every day.

SOMETIMES (Sonnet J)

Sometimes,

We go through trials—

That's why we have to keep Jesus in mind.

Sometimes,

It seems that we can't get through,

And others won't help us,

To do what we must do.

But, Jesus will never leave you alone;

The devil will tell you

That your Jesus is gone.

That's when faith and hope begin;

He'll be there on time,

Until the very end.

SOMETIMES (Sonnet K)

Sometimes,

I think about how much there is to fear;

Then I realize how my God is still here.

Sometimes,

I ponder over whatever might be;

Then I realize how much He's done for me.

God Almighty, one in three—

He is the source of my abilities.

He created the world,

And all that dwells therein;

Each day He awakens me,

To a new beginning.

Lord of the world, who died for me—

I thank Him for each victory.

Jesus' love fills my heart,

And walks with me daily—

We will never part.

SOMETIMES (Sonnet L)

Sometimes,

Life doesn't seem to go our way;

But Christ is risen and here to stay.

Sometimes,

We worry when we should have faith;

Sometimes it seems that there's no escape.

That's when we pray,

And ask God for strength,

And in His strength,

He will make a way.

So, cry for a moment,

But not too long—

For God will help us

To be very strong.

SOMETIMES (Sonnet M)

Sometimes,

Something may hurt you;

But God will let you see

The good of your hurt;

Whether it's losing a loved one,

Or breaking from an unhealthy relationship—

He will console you,

Until hurt becomes your victory.

Sometimes,

Things seem unbearable,

But He knows how much we can bear;

And when we learn to trust Him,

We'll find out that He is always there.

INSPIRATIONS THAT COME FROM THE MORNING VIEW

www.ingramcontent.com/pod-product-compliance
Lightning Source LLC
Chambersburg PA
CBHW040330300426
44113CB00020B/2711